NIGHTTIME ON THE OTHER SIDE OF EVERYTHING

NIGHTTIME ON THE OTHER SIDE OF EVERYTHING

SARAH KOBRINSKY

New Rivers Press is a nonprofit literary press associated with Minnesota State University Moorhead.

Cover and interior design by Kelsey Curfman
Author photo by Bart Nagel
The publication of *Nighttime on the Other Side of Everything* is made possible by the generous support of Minnesota State University Moorhead, the Dawson Family Endowment, and other contributors to New Rivers Press.

NRP Staff: Nayt Rundquist, Managing Editor; Kevin Carollo, Editor; Travis Dolence, Director; Trista Conzemius, Art Director
Interns: Trevor Fellows, Laura Grimm, Kendra Johnson, Anna Landsverk, Mikaila Norman, Lauren Phillips, Ashley Thorpe, Cameron Shulz, Rachael Wing
Nighttime on the Other Side of Everything book team: Evonne Eichhorn, Allison Funk, Logan Peterson, Zepherian Richardson, Maddie Schmidt

 Printed in the USA on acid-free, archival-grade paper.

Nighttime on the Other Side of Everything is distributed nationally by Small Press Distribution.

 New Rivers Press
c/o MSUM
1104 7th Ave S
Moorhead, MN 56563
www.newriverspress.com

For Jered and Jack

Contents

I.

Forger's Tremor 1
Milkman 2
Bento 3
Joke's on You 4
The Moonshining Place 5
Nostalgia Americana 6
No Parking 7
The Great Pace 8
Jesus Smokes 9
Eulogy 11
Hot Wings 12
A Poem for John who Writes in Elevens 13
Stick it in the Fridge 14
Intelligent Design 15
The Upside of Ipswich 16
Elf-Portrait 17
Failed Poem 18
Poem in Which You Get to Swear Like a Sailor 19
Nuts to That! 20

II.

The Turning Over 25
The Lady in Red Sauce 26
Lady-o-plasty 27
My Backward Lady 28
Softly She Slips 29
Ruffled 30
Claudine Takes the Cake 31
After the Dinner 32
Good for What Ails You 33
Safe Word 34
Whodunit? 35
In Every Bedroom 36
We must have been beautiful 37
You Don't Have to Call Me Darlin', Darlin' 38
Imagining William Carlos Williams in Bed 39

Old Wives' Tail   40
In Vitro   41
Number Nine   42
Afterbirth   43
Dripping   44
Wean   45
Paz   46

III.

Let's Set Our Differences Aside   49
Dowry   50
Domestic Violence   51
Memento   52
Aftershock   53
Rain   54
I Do   55
X & Y Have Another Fight   56
Divorce Settlement   57
After August   58
Siren   59
The Disciple   60
Below Stairs   61
The Trouble with Traveling Backwards   62
Practice Makes Perfect   63
Poker Face   64
Selfless Service   65
Aware Wolf   66
Supine   67
Kerosene kiss   68
Without You   69
The Dance Of Words   70
Anniversary   71
Again   72

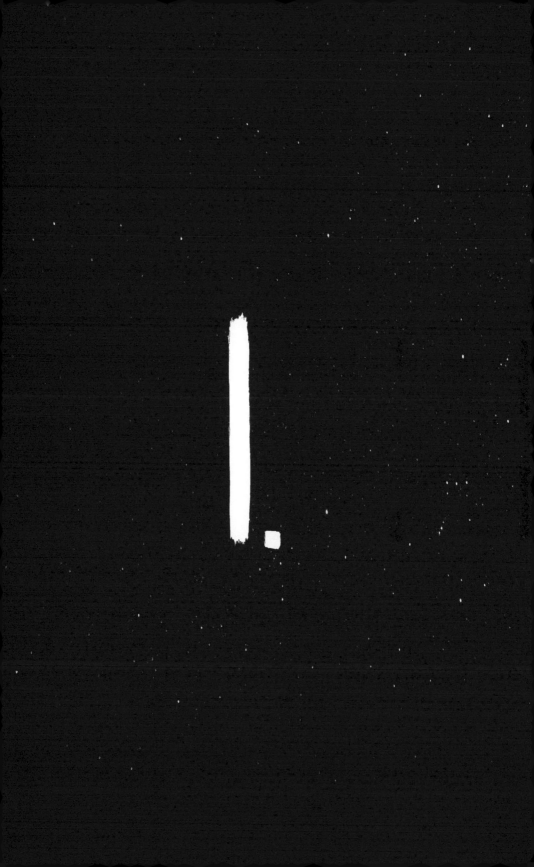

Forger's Tremor

If you look closely enough—
through a magnifying glass, perhaps,
or under a microscope—you will see,
from the uncertainty of the letters
inside these painstakingly selected words,
this poem was not written by me.

Milk Man

There is a white man in white clothes
who drives a white van
from house to white house—
each decently apart
with a perfect white fence.

He delivers the milk, the fresh white milk,
then takes the empties away.

Did he sleep with your mother?
Did he sleep with my mother?
Does he look like me?

He is full of milk, creamy white milk,
fresh from the parish condensery.
His teeth are white, reflective white—
The better to see yourself in me!

And all the white ladies
look out their white-veiled windows
at the white man entering all the other
white houses, hotly they blush
before turning green—

White trousers down around
white skinny ankles, white-knuckle coupling
on white Formica tables where later
they will feed their husbands
little white lies.

Then the white man drives away
in his milky white van to the next cul-de-sac
on the other side of town.
His job here is done.
Everyone has what they need.

Did he sleep with your mother?
Does he look like me?

Bento

after Christopher Middleton

To lift the roof off a doll's house
To stuff each room with foodstuffs
To have a place for everything

To have everything in place
To pace each room on wooden stilts
To browse the house like a thief

To steal your way into the bedroom
To ponder what to pilfer first
To strip the bed of dirty sheets

To keep coming back for more
To dip the baby in the bathwater
To leave towels on the floor

To lift timber limbs to lips
To stuff your mouth with foodstuffs
To place everything you have

Inside your picket fence

Jokes on You

Steals the pie cooling in your window,

Toilet papers your house

And the trees in your front yard,

Eggs your car, short sheets your bed,

Tapes *Kick Me!* to your back

Then snaps your bra strap,

Puts your hands in warm water

And makes you pee in your sleep,

Plastic wraps your toilet seat,

Ties your shoelaces together,

Loosens the lid of your salt n' pepper shaker,

Absconds with your clothes

When you skinny dip in the lake—

Love rings your doorbell and runs away.

The Moonshining Place

At the edge of the city,
at the edge of the world,
at the edge between
the earth and endless sky,
the moonshining place,

the place where we hung
our long summer legs
over the edge to fight
the urge to drop a shoe
or sneak a real first kiss,

the place where we played
hide-and-go-seek
and *Tag, you're it!* until
we couldn't breathe
or the sun went down,

the place where we came
on the quietest nights,
to feel the moon kiss
the edge between
our skin and endless sky.

Nostalgia Americana

Am I a beauty queen, Johnny?
Luanne licked her lips
then clicked her compact shut.
Of course you are, darlin',
Johnny lied, his eyes darting
back and forth from her breasts
in the rearview mirror
to the long, barren road ahead.

No Parking

Motorcyclists always find
a great place to park,
an available slip
to narrowly escape.

You on the other hand—
despite your gold hoop
and your GPS—
have nowhere to go.

You drift aimlessly
in your boathouse
and your bathrobe,
holding fast to the wheel,

Captain of your own fate,
tired and fat
in this downtown
landing pad—

The cement persists:
Your anchor is no good here.

The Great Pace

With a firm hand and an outstretched arm,
You delivered us from Egypt.
-from the Passover Haggadah

When you weren't sweating or shitting,
when you weren't in bed, a baby again,
between Mom and Dad shaking,
Mom and Dad taking turns to dunk you
in the tub all night to keep you cool,
when you weren't pleading for death,
when you weren't begging us
to put you out of your misery like a dog,

You were pacing, pacing with an energy
none of us had ever known, pacing
around the house in your bathrobe
and your FBI sunglasses, pacing
with the weight of the junk
still in your veins, pacing
in your Levis and your sticky bare feet.

And you were mambling under your breath,
mambling, that was your word,
prayers that made sense only for you:
If she isn't crazy, you better check her for nuts!
Hey dollface, wanna take a ride?

When the speed of your feet wasn't enough,
the house too small to chase or runaway
from what we'll never know, you fueled up
the John Deere and drove down to the river,
back and forth and back and forth,
there was nothing left to mow.

My brother, with a firm hand
and an outstretched arm, the rubber tightening
around your bicep for the last time,
you were delivered.

Jesus Smokes

My father, the cancer doctor, sits at the head of the table
coughing like his father, a cancer doctor, coughed
in the oxygen tent in the room in the hospital in Canada.

My grandfather, a Russian immigrant famous for his Anglophilia,
leaned out of his oxygen tent with his riding crop
and whispered through cancerous spittle.

My son, you must become a doctor.

My father, who didn't want to become a doctor,
sits at the head of the table coughing up white smoke.

It's Passover and everyone's on their third glass of wine.
In his best Rabbi Burkle voice, my father chants a blessing, then says:

Jesus smokes.

Now, the Jesus reference is weird because we're Jewish,
but my father, the cancer doctor, he's famous for saying things
that are weird like: *Jesus smokes.*

Myself and my five siblings, all confirmed smokers,
and our mother, an ex-smoker,
sit around our father, the non-smoker, smoking…

Our father, the cancer doctor, who likes to be referred to as
the Blood Count, clears his throat and looks upon our ashen faces:

*Just as Jesus died for the people's sins,
I cough for my children's smoke.
Jesus smokes.*

Our father, the Jewish doctor, sits at the head of the table
and chants another blessing:

My children, you must never become doctors.

So my sister, the chain smoker, and my mother, the ex-smoker,
and my brother, the social smoker, and my eldest brother,
the I'm-so-broke-I-roll-my-own smoker,
and my youngest brother, the chronic pot smoker,
and my other brother,
the I-just-quit-so-can-I-have-one-of-yours smoker,
and me, the I-feel-so-guilty-because-I-smoke smoker,
all agree to never become doctors.

Our father, the would-be witch doctor, sits at the head of the table
and instructs us, in his bathrobe, to pour the fourth glass of wine:

Blessed are you, Ruler of the Universe, who doctored the fruit of the vine.

And for a moment, none of us are smoking.
Elijah's wind moves through the room and everything is silent.

Our father, the cancer doctor, sits at the head of the table,
laughing like his father, the cancer doctor, laughed when he heard the news
he was going to have a son who might—*God willing*—
be a doctor someday.

Jesus smokes.

Eulogy

I read, graveside, the story of your life
from a handful of badly strewn words.
          I haven't got much to say.
My friend, you were always more dead
          in life than you are now.

Hot Wings

1.

All-You-Can-Eat
every Wednesday night
for $9.95. Celery sticks
and a plastic ramekin
full of blue cheese
in each basket.

2.

Icarus, you dumbass.

A Poem for John Who Writes in Elevens

for John Oliver Simon

There are eleven syllables in this line—
eleven eleven, my dear, make a wish!
This is also a *Dear John* letter, dear John,
but not *that* kind of a *Dear John* letter, John.

I just wanted to feel your form, try you on,
count and count again the stars in Joseph's dream.
Did you see any stars when you were under?
Are you any lighter now that growth is gone?

Once I heard of a man who kept his tumor
on his mantle in a jar next to his wife.
He wished on it, like on a star, called it John.

Stick It in the Fridge

I am a hundred years
behind the times. I just
started using electricity.
Remember that thing
we swore we would
never let spoil? You know—
our love? Good news.
Stick it in the fridge.

Intelligent Design

There's a phantom pain in my long-lost tail,
the same in my umbilical button.
They tied me once to my mother and further
to the first ever monkey
             who stood on his own two feet.

I pick up my gorilla suit from the cleaners,
an analgesic, then stand on the corner
distracting traffic. A sign around the neck
of my new skin says:
             Will work like a dog for bananas.

The Upside of Ipswich

I have never been there,
But some people have.
It can't be that bad, right?

Elf-Portrait

My candy-striped tights are too tight.
The toes of my shoes long to unfurl
into the jovial length of a clown's.
My hands, as tiny as child factory
workers', are tired of the details:
zippers, buttons, eyes fastened with glue.
I don't always love what I do. But *I do.*
I make. I tinker. I create. An instinct born
of my blueprints, deep within my DNA.
With every breath, I feel the first
of my kind hitting hammer against nail.
I am not destined for idleness.
If I tried, I would fail.

Failed Poem

In Sligotown
the water runs yellow,
stained from the secrets
of the pilgrims there—

All the failed poems
for the dead poet,
the piss
from the elusive
Innisfree.

Poem in Which You Get to Swear Like a Sailor

You!

[point finger]

Why I oughta!

[shake fist]

And another thing . . .

[raise voice]

How dare you!

[stamp foot]

Go fuck yourself!

[puff chest]

Asshole.

[slam door]

Nuts to That!

after Speakeasy SF

Through the grandfather clock,

through the looking glass,

behind closed doors, under wraps.

Be careful, the walls have ears.

No, really. The walls have ears.

See over there? That mirror.

Pick up the receiver. What do you hear?

The still small voice of your heart

sure speaks easy, no? The voice

that says, *I coulda been somebody!*

Like that giant Gianini. Well,

in this gin joint you are somebody.

We won't stifle the likes

of Gustav Eiffel or any ordinary guy

chasing after the American dream,

holding out his empty hands

for the next sawbuck, the next big win,

the next big ship to come in.

Through the grandfather clock,

through the highball glass,

inside coat pockets, at the craps,

a bottle of hooch with just enough burn

but won't make you blind.

On the contrary, it'll make you see

you're still in the game, still going strong,

your hopes and dreams distilled

into one moment, one card, one chip—

double down, double down

and then it's gone.

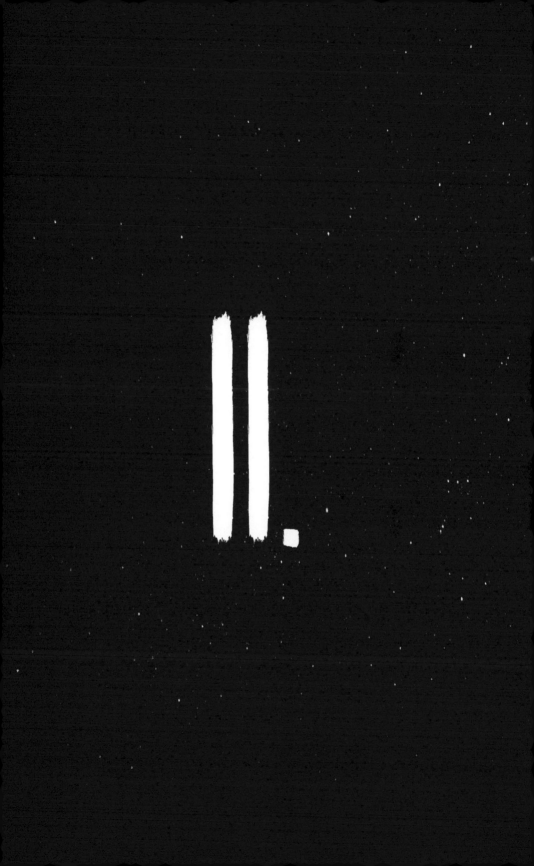

II.

The Turning Over

In Rutherford I root and rummage
through garbage, rotten newspaper,
        prescription plums.

An old woman watches closely,
she has seen this dance before,
        the turning over of

ordinary things: a pair of shoes,
worn receipts, an empty suitcase,
        a rusty icebox.

She knows this dance by heart,
the urgent search for the story
        on the other side,

the stunned eye of the surprise,
answers, fleshy meat of the matter,
        another reason why.

Tirelessly I turn, still she watches,
every back, every bottom, the quiet
        maker and her mark.

The Lady in Red Sauce

Everyone knows not to have spaghetti on the first date
but she can't help herself. She loves men
who like to watch women eat.

Not the fat-lady-fetish type, but the hardworking kind—
lovers who like to knead the bread
in order to find the bones.

Lady-o-plasty

Frances told them she had it done
after she birthed her third child.

It felt, she said, like twirling
a pencil in a cave. But the truth is

she hated her own asymmetry,
how one pink lip was bigger than

the other, darker too, how it peeked
through her fleshy shell like

a curious turtle's head. She changed
her breasts and most of her

face as well. You can't read her
reasons for anything now—

There is no tell when your pout
is frozen forever. Next she'll have

her teeth, her hair, even her asshole,
bleached for good measure.

You can never be too beautiful,
too clean, or too white.

My Backward Lady

Remove her dainty tea gloves,
Her handbag and her hat.

Take away her underthings—
Bloomers, slips, sundry whatnots.

Deepen the lines in her aging face.
Stain her teeth a feral yellow.

Play her your gramophone
To rough the edges of her words.

Make her repeat *Fuck*
Until it comes out of her naturally,

Not at will, but beyond will—
Instinctive and necessary as breath.

Watch her hair grow wild and grizzly.
Desiccate her lips and the tracts of her skin.

Steal her from the Ladies Lunch
And drop her at the bar.

Let the drinking begin here. Early.
Show her a new kind of music,

Lead her downtown, where
Sirens sing the arias in the streets.

Teach her to stumble on sharp stiletto heels.
Let her trip until she stays down.

So deliciously low, so horribly dirty,
The angels would weep for her

Cold face, cold hands, cold feet.
Oh, wouldn't it be lovely?

Wouldn't it?

Softly She Slips

Softly she slips from crinolines,
petticoats and pantyhose,
slips crooked wings from perfect bone,
slips again into membrane, fine
nightdress of solidified tears,
slips once more into bed sheets, tangles,
untangles, and finally falls asleep.

You see, at night she has no need for wings,
no forces to fly against, only dreams
where everything is just as it is
and never slips away.

Ruffled

She sleeps backwards
from morning to night

with her head
on inside-out pillows

at the crippled foot
of her upside-down bed.

Claudine Takes the Cake

Muscles it out of the pan
impatiently, a sharp ache
surfaces in her smile.
The corners of her mouth
crack as she takes a bite.
Her heart tilts on its axis.
The floor trembles—
something from Brahms.
That bastard, she sighs,
then nothing but crumbs.

After Dinner

I want you to pull this tablecloth
from underneath our conversation,
leaving the candlesticks untouched.

I want you to wipe away the remains,
all the silverware, the dinner plates,
with your forearm and your elbow.

When this commotion is not enough,
and all the wax has dripped to the wood,
I want you to take me, take me

Take me back four million years
till I'm on all fours with my hands
and knees digging into the earth.

I want to swing from your body
till my wrists grow numb,
my hands no longer dexterous.

We'll take back all the trees,
every fold and curve of the canopy,
we'll wrestle beneath one skin.

All the fishes, the lizards, will hide
in the dirt turned up from our heels,
they'll blush at our unruly haste.

Oh no, there's no stopping now!
Our hands will be turning,
turning back time until . . .

BANG! We are all that there is.
The beginning of the universe.
No natural law. No natural cause.

Good for What Ails You

Wear red. Wear more red.
And when you're sick of red,
Fuck it! Wear nothing at all.
Flaunt the organic spinach
between your teeth. Eat meat.
Get books from the library,
leave secrets in the margins—
dark ones, funny ones—
for someone else to read.
Learn how to hula, lambada,
then forget those fancy steps
and just dance. Go on, shake it.
Kiss everyone who moves you.
If not with your beefy lips,
then at least with your smile.

Safe Word

When the pleasure that is
also pain becomes only pain,

when you are too close to the mouth
of what you are most afraid of,

when you have simply gone too far
and might never come back,

when there is just enough breath,
you say, *Rumpelstiltskin.*

Whodunit?

1.

Ms. Scarlet
in the bathroom
with a tampon.

2.

Colonel Mustard
in the kitchen
with a chicken leg.

3.

Professor Plum
in the library
with my thesis.

4.

Mrs. White
in the bedroom
with her smile.

In Every Bedroom

In every bedroom where lovers whisper
and dream the future without fear,

under the beds of the fallen,
fluttering my wings to help them rise up,

in the closet, an old forgotten suit,
ready to protect at the drop of a lonely hat,

beneath the creaky floorboards covered
in sweaty strewn clothes,

in the ceiling fan, spinning ease wherever
love is a possibility,

in the sink and mirror, anywhere lovers
groom and prepare for one another,

in the moment before every first kiss
and the sweet memory of it after,

in the corners of every bedroom where
the echoes of laughter hide,

in the eyes of the tired lovers—
through her breath, into his heart, I arrive.

We must have been beautiful
to let all that light in
unembarrassed

You Don't Have to Call Me Darlin', Darlin'*

You were there where the bones came together.
        You made my body move when nothing else would.

You flew a red balloon outside my bedroom window.
        You plumped up my pillows to resuscitate my dreams.

You carved our other names into an oak tree in the park.
        You brought me cold water. You cleared away the dark.

You lifted the oil stains from the work shirt of my life.
        You trimmed my mustache. You called me your wife.

*Title is from the song "You Never Even Called Me by My Name" by David Alan Coe.

Imagining William Carlos Williams in Bed

He makes love to her
He makes love
to her. He makes
love to her

Old Wives' Tail

As wide as an ax handle,
fat gathered and stored
like cherished letters
on sturdy bone, not from
a lifetime of idleness
or endless unmet hungers,
but from our deeper longing
for something soft, to dull
the sharp edges of loss—
a pillow for your throne.

In Vitro

Mother Instinct kicks in.
I want to breastfeed,
It's kind of sick.
All these fertilized eggs,
Baby, which one will stick?

Number Nine

after Sylvia Plath

I'm going the whole nine yards, baby!
A beehive, honey, a Russian doll.
My stores are stocked, bursting, for winter,
A big fat Fräulein dressed to the nines.
Good and stuffed like sausage or peppers,
A clumsy nymph crawling on cloud nine.
The powers of nine muses are mine,
The longed-for prize after the bull's eye:
Nine times out of ten, I get it right.

Afterbirth

I didn't eat the placenta
or bury it under a tree.
I don't know where it is.
Maybe in a biohazard bag
somewhere in a landfill
full of other biohazard bags
with countless needles,
tumors, spleens. But one
thing I do know for sure—
the kid is here with me.

Dripping

Happy mothers sit
in a circle feeding babies,
accidentally dripping
breast milk
into each other's coffee.

How wonderful life is!
So unpredictable and sweet.

Wean

Where does the old milk go?
Is it absorbed back into the body,
back into the cells? Does it become
blood or breath or other sustenance?
Is it really gone? How do I know?
Go ahead, friend, milk me.

Paz

Even though
his eyes
never opened
and his lungs
never felt
the powerful
rush of air,
he was still
born.

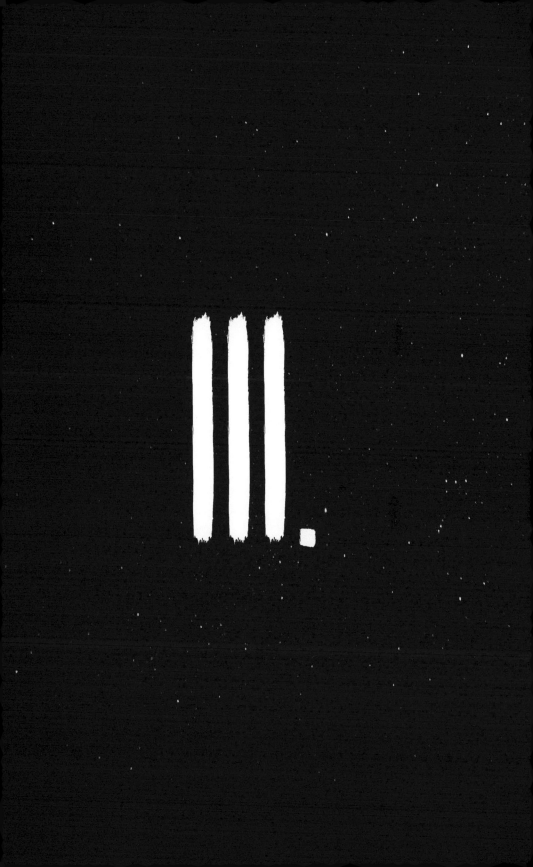

III.

Let's Set Our Differences Aside

Let's arrive at the Truth.
Whoever gets there first should send
The other one a postcard:
A beach scene, a cobblestone street,
A city skyline alive at night.
Darling, I am here.
How I wish you were beautiful!

Dowry

after Michael Armitage

He turns her upside down,

shakes her naked body

to get every last penny,

to count the change,

to see what she is worth.

He shakes her harder still

to turn her inside out,

to see what other secrets

fall from hidden pockets.

Her body is his broom,

her hair sweeps up the mess

of her own fallen treasure

into a shapeless pile

where her feet once stood.

Domestic Violence

Her face reminded him
of the red velvet cake
she made that night.
It was all he could do
to keep from—

Memento

Whenever that voice returns,
the voice of the flattened
flower she used to be

between his books,
between his outbursts,
between the sheets,

whenever she places
blame upon herself,
upon her body

in the very places
his hands used to be,
she reads the police report.

Aftershock

In another time and place,
we are better people.

No one lies. The Earth
never shakes.

Somewhere else,
we are stronger still—

When we say we are sorry,
we honestly mean it.

Rain

The smell of jasmine and wet cement

The smell of rotten leaves and uncertainty

The smell of *I told you so*

The smell of *You should've known better*

The smell of *I could've been a contender*

The smell of *Honey, let's think it over*

The smell of newspaper

The smell of rain

I Do

Two people sit across from each other at a late night café.
They are tired and have nothing to say. Sometime ago,
in their uneventful history, they made an unspoken vow
to live within this emptiness, this boredom, together.
Anything to stave off the quiet terror of being alone.
Now here they are, staring out at different vistas—
one toward the City, the other toward the Sea.

X & Y Have Another Fight

Meanwhile
down the road
the local taco truck
blares *La Cucaracha*
beautifully out of tune.

Divorce Settlement

A handful of bills
on the bedside table.
You were good enough
not to wake me. Still,
I cannot sleep for love
or money, certainly
not for yours. I leave it
all uncounted before
I knock it to the floor.

After August

is September,

almost over—

pause—

What next?

Comes October,

mean October,

not as mean

as you, August.

Then November

and December,

cold and hard

but no match

for you, August.

Over now—

pause—

What next?

No, really,

I insist.

After you.

No, after *You*,

August.

Siren

The candle burning
while you're gone,
the oven still on,
and the door—
you know you closed it,
but is it locked?

The Disciple

The disciple sits in his heavy robes thumbing
his makeshift mala—a string of Mardi Gras beads
leftover from the last night of his other life.
He tries hard to do nothing about the numbness
in his feet or the itch at the tip of his nose.

With all of his focus on his breath, he cannot breathe.
He feels as if his lungs are caving in, he wants to scream—
though from the outside, on the surface, he looks like a saint.
Lightheaded, almost faint, he lifts his inner gaze
from his chest to his throat. The disciple begins to choke.

He swallows and swallows, trying to keep it all down—
everything he left unuttered and undone.
The gaudy beads slip from his hands to the ground,
but he will not budge to retrieve them.
He is committed to this stillness. Even if it kills him.

Below Stairs

When we wake, dreams fall from our bodies
and gather at our feet—humble servants bowed
so low in their humility, they become invisible. Yet
they stay with us through our days, eager to please
and obey, a feeling we can never quite shake—
if only we would let ourselves see them.

The Trouble with Traveling Backwards

Your hair blows over
your ears into your eyes,
the punch line arrives
long before the joke,
the dog tears at the meat,
then he begs—
your heart breaks
before you have a chance
to fall in love.

Practice Makes Perfect

Deliberately I fail, then move on
        to the next mistake,
to grow humbler, to wear old skin
        from my knees.

And some days I almost get it right—
        by accident or not—
I kiss the earth anyway to keep
        my spirits limber.

Poker Face

My third eye sees your third eye
And raises an eyebrow.

Selfless Service

That's what they call it,
but we know better.
At the ashram, everyone
has a chore to do.
Some scrub vegetables
or toilets, others clean
the altar or iron
Swami's underwear.
But me? I've got it easy.
In my last life,
I did something right—
All I have to do is
make the tea.

Aware Wolf

Let's call him Phil. Phil teaches yoga.
All his students say,
"My, what tight yoga pants you have!"
"The better to do downward dog,"
he bows with his paws in prayer.

He goes to the farmers market
to get groceries for the week.
All the vendors say,
"Gee, what sharp teeth you have!"
"The better to eat locally-sourced,
grass-fed organic meat," he says.

In the evening, he sits in the park
to watch his predatory thoughts,
to watch the sun go down.
All the people say,
"Phil, what still haunches you have!"
"The better to do nothing with."

Supine

She lies down,

plays dead.

Her fists unfold

into stars, palms up,

her legs drift apart—

toes roll out

to the sides,

repose.

She breathes.

Wind blows

beneath her skin,

against her bones,

a place for everything

to enter, a place

for everything

to go.

Kerosene Kiss

for Jered

Grease caught
in cracks of fingers,
smell of leather
on toughened skin—
animal-soft
in smoky light,
tobacco blessings
on earthen bed,
lips upon whispers
hush the night.

Without You

I am a dancer with no feet,
a statesman with no tongue,
a thinker with no thumb
or forefinger
to rub against my chin.

The Dance of Words

When my hand leaves your shoulder,
      I turn to dust.
We have lived within and without the Word,
      for each other,
in the black stretch and curl
      of the letters,
and outside in the great white void
      binding them together.
You said, in a whisper, *Don't be afraid.*

Anniversary

It was the coldest
that day had ever been
on record. You got
frostbite carrying me
into the reception—
the first of many
beautiful scars
that are ours
and ours alone.

Again

A question that

answers itself

without question,

without reason,

without ever

being asked.

Acknowledgements

I am grateful to the following journals and publications that included my poems.

Bay Area Generations: "Dripping," "Good for What Ails you," "Lady-o-plasty," "Wean"

Eleven Eleven: "Claudine Takes the Cake," "Forger's Tremor"

Jewish Quarterly, UK: "Jesus Smokes"

Magma Poetry: "You Don't Have to Call Me Darlin', Darlin'"

One Sentence Poems: "Poker Face"

Poems on the Emery-Go-Round: "Aware Wolf"

Red Light Lit: "After Dinner," "Kerosene Kiss," "The Lady in Red Sauce," "Safe Word," "We must have been beautiful"

Rising (UK): "Dripping," "Jesus Smokes," "My Backward Lady," "Ruffled"

Shampoo Poetry: "Let's Set Our Differences Aside," "Rain"

Sparkle + Blink: "Jesus Smokes"

Wild Quarterly: "Selfless Service"

Writing without Walls: "Lady-o-plasty," "My Blackward Lady," "Whodunit?"

82 Review: "The Trouble with Traveling Backwards"

About the Author

Sarah Kobrinsky was the 2013-2015 Poet Laureate of Emeryville, California. She was born in Canada, raised in North Dakota, seasoned in England, and tempered in California. Sarah and her husband have a handmade dinnerware company called Jered's Pottery.

ABOUT NEW RIVERS PRESS

New Rivers Press emerged from a drafty Massachusetts barn in winter 1968. Intent on publishing work by new and emerging poets, founder C.W. "Bill" Truesdale labored for weeks over an old Chandler & Price letterpress to publish three hundred fifty copies of Margaret Randall's collection So Many Rooms Has a House but One Roof. About four hundred titles later, New Rivers is now a nonprofit learning press, based since 2001 at Minnesota State University Moorhead. Charles Baxter, one of the first authors with New Rivers, calls the press "the hidden backbone of the American literary tradition."

As a learning press, New Rivers guides student editors, designers, writers, and filmmakers through the various processes involved in selecting, editing, designing, publishing, and distributing literary books. In working, learning, and interning with New Rivers Press, students gain integral real-world knowledge that they bring with them into the publishing workforce at positions with publishers across the country, or to begin their own small presses and literary magazines.

Please visit our website: newriverspress.com for more information.